MEDIEVAL KNIGHTS

DAVID NICOLLE

Acknowledgements

The publishers would like to thank Bill Donohoe and Terry Gabbey, who illustrated the see-through scenes; James Field, who illustrated the cover; and the individuals and organizations that have given their permission to reproduce the following pictures:

Ancient Art & Architecture Collection: 11 top left, 16 top left, 36 top right, 37 top right.
Antikvarisk-Topografiska-Arkivet: 35 centre right.
Biblioteca Apostolica Vaticana: 4 below right.
Bibliothéque Nationale, Paris: 17 centre right.
Board of Trustees of the Royal Armouries: 29 bottom right.
Bodleian Library, Oxford: 35 bottom right.
British Library: 14 top left, 31 bottom right (both), 44 top left.
Crown copyright: reproduction by permission of Historic Scotland: 45 top right.
J. Allan Cash: 27 top left, 37 centre left. **Michael Dixon:** 43 centre right. **Edinburgh University Library, Kelvingrove:** 38 bottom right, 39 top right.
Glasgow Museums & Art Gallery: 45 bottom right.
Kremlin: 38 bottom left. **Kunsthistorisches Museum, Wien:** 7 top left (both).
Masters & Fellows of Trinity College, Cambridge: 9 top right.
Michael Holford: 25 top right. **Museo d'Arte de Barcelona:** 41 top right.
National Museum, Budapest: 12 bottom right.
The Pierpont Morgan Library: 34 top left.
Scala: 7 top right, 10 bottom right, 15 centre left, 19 bottom right, 19 bottom left, 20 bottom right, 22 bottom right, 23 top right, 23 bottom right, 27 bottom right, 43 bottom left.
Sonia Halliday: 30 top left, 32 centre right. **Southampton City Heritage Services:** 27 top right.
Warburg-Stiflung: 21 top right. **Dr D. Winfield:** 28 bottom right.

Illustrators:
Jonathan Adams: icons, 5, 12, 18, 26 top, 29. **James Field (Simon Girling):** cover.
Terry Gabbey (Associated Freelance Artists): 6, 7, 13 bottom, 19, 22, 30, 31, 35.
André Hrydziuszko: 6 top, 15 bottom, 16 bottom, 38. **Angus McBride (Linden Artists):** title page, 4, 13 top, 14, 15, 26-27, 28, 34, 39, 42, 44-45, 46-47. **Mike White:** 10-11, 16-17, 20, 21, 36, 37, 43.

Editors: Andrew Farrow and Alyson Jones
Designers: Anthony Godber and Nick Avery
Picture Researcher: Thelma Gilbert
Production Controller: Lorraine Stebbing

Other titles in this series:
The Aztecs, Ancient Rome, Ancient Greece, Ancient Egypt, The Middle Ages, The Renaissance, The Vikings, The Age of Industry, Forts & Castles, Tombs & Treasure, The Celts, Plains Indians, Houses & Homes, Submarines & Ships, The Apaches & Pueblo Peoples of the Southwest, Ancient China, The Wild West, The Incas, Ancient Wonders

First published in Great Britain in 1997 by Heinemann Children's Reference,
an imprint of Heinemann Educational Publishers,
Halley Court, Jordan Hill, Oxford, OX2 8EJ,
a division of Reed Educational & Professional Publishing Ltd.

MADRID ATHENS PARIS
FLORENCE PORTSMOUTH NH CHICAGO
SAO PAULO SINGAPORE TOKYO
MELBOURNE AUCKLAND IBADAN
GABORONE JOHANNESBURG KAMPALA NAIROBI

ISBN 0 600 58884 X

A CIP catalogue record for this book is available at the British Library.

See-through pages printed by SMIC, France.
Books printed and bound in Italy.

CONTENTS

MYTHS AND LEGENDS

<big>M</big>ost people think of the Middle Ages as a time of brave warriors and heroic knights in shining armour, killing dragons and rescuing damsels in distress. This book is not about legendary heroes, but real knights – ordinary men trying to do what they thought was right. These knights were members of a special class dedicated to fighting for their king, for Christianity, for their country or simply for justice.

In the story of Sir Gawain and the Green Knight, Gawain chops off the giant's head in a duel, but it does not kill him. Once winter is over, the giant returns, carrying his head under his arm, to take his single blow at the head of Gawain as agreed. Like a true knight, Gawain keeps his promise and prepares to meet the giant's challenge.

SIR GAWAIN

Typical of the medieval stories about knights is the tale of Sir Gawain and the Green Knight, which is one of the tales of King Arthur and his Knights of the Round Table. In it, the young knight Sir Gawain is challenged to a duel by a giant Green Knight. He says Gawain can have the first blow. However, if Gawain fails to kill him, he will return in a year for his own blow at Gawain. Gawain cuts off the Green Knight's head – then is astounded to find out that the Green Knight is a magical creature, who picks up his head, declaring he will return in a year's time!

THE GREEN KNIGHT RETURNS

When the Green Knight returns, Gawain stands ready to receive his blow. This proves he is a brave knight who keeps his promise even though it will cause his death. Gawain, as a true knight, believes that honour is more important than life itself. The Green Knight respects Gawain's behaviour and so lets him live.

This medieval manuscript shows Crusader knights besieging the great city of Antioch in 1098. The popular view of medieval knights is of brave warriors in shining armour, who were polite to women and respected a brave foe. In reality, knights were just like other soldiers.

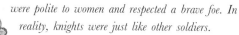

This map shows the main Christian states in Europe in about AD 1270, and their main neighbours, the Islamic nations to the south and southeast and the Mongol Golden Horde to the east. By the end of the Middle Ages, Europeans had a clearer idea what the rest of the world contained. Far-travelling merchants even knew about China and perhaps Japan.

LEGENDARY HEROES

Where did these stories of knights and magical creatures come from? In the Middle Ages, there were no radios, televisions or films. Instead, poems and songs were used to entertain people. Some of the most imaginative stories were written at this time. Medieval minstrels told tales of the heroism of the knights, and, of course, exaggerated the deeds of their heroes to make the stories more entertaining.

MYTH AND REALITY

Some of these stories show that most Europeans thought the rest of the world was a frightening and hostile place. This was mainly because they knew so little about it. They saw brave knights as Christendom's main defence against the unknown world.

Encouraged by the Church, knights went on Crusades, fighting Muslims and other non-Christians. They often travelled widely. Some brave or desperate men even fought beyond the frontiers of Christian Europe. As a result, more information about other parts of the world gradually filtered back to Europe. Although they feared their neighbours, medieval Europeans were also willing to learn about them and respect them. In the *chansons de geste*, epic and heroic songs sung by medieval minstrels, for example, Muslim Saracen soldiers were often described as 'knights', just like those of western Europe.

THE DECLINE OF KNIGHTHOOD

The knights played a great part in changing the European view of the medieval world. Gradually, however, western European civilization itself changed, and the knight in armour, as well as the old ideals of knighthood, became outdated and slowly disappeared.

This map shows how most European people viewed the world in about AD 1095. Christendom was a small part of the medieval world and often felt threatened by its neighbours. Information about these peoples slowly filtered back to Europe, but almost always made these mysterious kingdoms seem much more powerful than they really were. Many people still believed that terrifying sea monsters and strange half-human creatures lived on the edges of the world.

5

THE FIRST KNIGHTS

The early knights lived in castles like the early 11th-century upper fortress which stood in Rüdesheim in Germany.

THE FIRST KNIGHTS

In the late 8th century, a new 'Western Roman Empire' was created by Charlemagne, king of the Franks. To build and defend his new empire, Charlemagne needed thousands of well-trained professional soldiers. At the very top of his army were 'milites'. These were armoured cavalrymen who were in many ways the first knights of medieval Europe. The armies led by Charlemagne and his successors were also the only ones able to defeat the Vikings who raided northwest Europe in the 9th and 10th centuries.

In the 5th century, the western half of the Roman Empire was destroyed by invading Germanic tribes. The only professional soldiers in the invading armies were a few warriors who protected their rulers. For nearly **400** years they were the most powerful soldiers in the west.

'Charles, King of the Franks... controlled Rome, where the ancient Caesars had always lived, as well as ruling many other parts of Italy, France and Germany. So, as God had given him these territories, it seemed right that he should also accept the title of Emperor when it was offered to him by all Christendom.'

— *The Lauresheim Chronicle* —

Charlemagne became emperor with the blessing of the Pope in Rome. He was the first western emperor since the fall of Rome, and his large, efficient army made him the equal of the only other 'great powers' in Europe – the Byzantine Empire in eastern Europe and the Muslim Caliphate of Spain.

The heavily armoured and highly mobile cavalry of Charlemagne's empire led the armies of his successors, the Carolingian and Ottonian emperors. They were the only soldiers able to defeat the Vikings who raided Europe from the north, the Hungarians who invaded from the east, and the Saracens who came from the south.

The early knights fought with spears and swords (right). Their armour usually consisted of mail, and iron helmets, like the one above.

CHARLEMAGNE'S MILITES

Charlemagne's cavalrymen wore mail armour, an iron helmet and carried a large wooden shield. They fought with a spear, sword and sometimes a bow. This equipment was so effective that it hardly changed for 300 years.

However, each miles and his powerful war-horses were very expensive. They had to live all over western Europe if they were to defend every area from invaders. They alone were able to defend the people of Christian western Europe from waves of Vikings, Magyar Hungarians and Mediterranean Muslim raiders who almost destroyed the huge and wealthy empire that Charlemagne had created.

THE NEW RULING CLASS

The only answer was to make each miles into a local landlord so that the peasants could feed him with their crops and pay him taxes. This changed the milites' position in society. They were no longer just soldiers. Instead they became an aristocracy, or ruling class.

This process took time because the existing earls, counts and other powerful nobles were not prepared to give up their privileges easily to these rough 'upstart' fighting men. In the end, however, the milites and the old nobility merged to become a new aristocracy – the knights.

THE NORMANS

Perhaps the most effective of the new knights were the Normans – who were themselves descended from a powerful group of Vikings who had settled in Normandy in north-west France. They learned much about warfare from Charlemagne's armies and won many battles through careful planning and daring attacks. They established states in southern Italy and Sicily, and conquered England and Ireland.

Many Normans also served in the Byzantine armies (see pages 28–29), and when Pope Urban II called for a crusade against the Muslims, Norman knights from France and Italy were at the forefront of the great armies that went to the Holy Land.

One of the most accurate and realistic pictures of a Carolingian warrior nobleman is on this small wall-painting (above) in Italy.

The Pope gives Charlemagne a splendidly decorated banner (below) as a sign that he has the Church's support.

ARMING A KNIGHT

Below, a late 12th-century knight and his son are being armed for battle, assisted by servants. Their armour basically consisted of mail – sheets of interlocking iron rings – mostly worn over some sort of quilted padding that absorbed the shock of a blow. When the see-through page is turned, they are shown almost ready for battle.

The arms and armour used by knights and other western European fighting men changed a great deal during the Middle Ages. However, from the earliest days, armour nearly always consisted of more than one layer. The first layer would be a pair of loose breeches and a shirt. Over the breeches the knight would wear hose, which were like two separate tight-fitting trouser-legs.

12TH CENTURY KNIGHTS

Over his hose, a 12th-century knight wore mail leggings, called chausses. Next, to cushion his armour, he would put on a padded coat called a gambeson. On top of this would be a tunic, probably very long as a mark of wealth and status.

12th CENTURY KNIGHTS

1 Breeches	6 Mail hauberk
2 Shirt	7 Coif over
3 Hose	padding
4 Mail chausses	8 Surcoat
5 Long tunic	9 Helmet

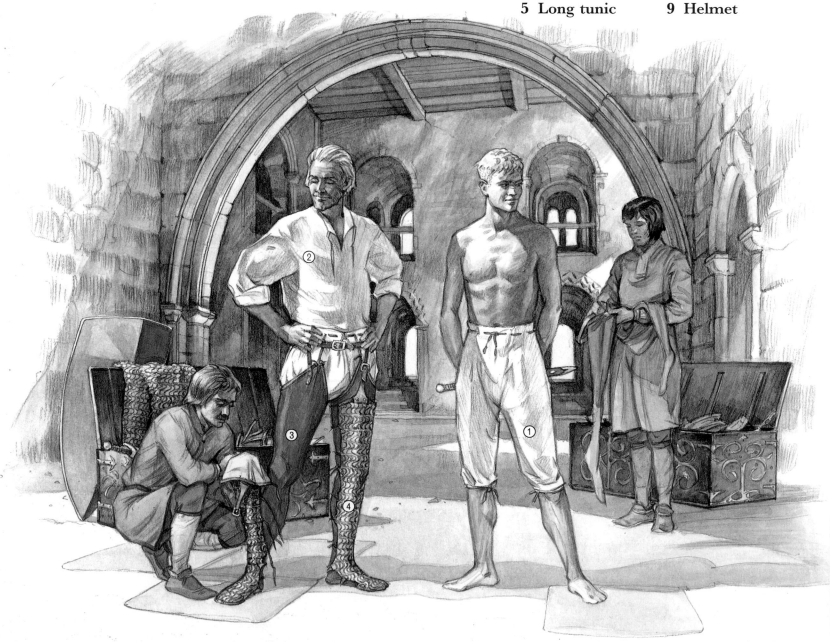

READY FOR BATTLE

The knight's main piece of armour was a mail shirt called a hauberk, which usually had a mail hood called a coif. The hauberk was very awkward to put on, but not as tiring to wear as it might seem. Over this would be worn a cloth surcoat.

Finally, the knight had a helmet to protect his head, and a large wooden shield. Armed with a heavy sword for cutting rather than stabbing, and a long lance, the knight was a dangerous enemy.

Below, two knights from around 1325–1350 are taking off their armour after a tournament. Although some of their armour still consists of mail, they also now wear more rigid coats-of-plate made of scales and small pieces of plate. When the see-through page is turned, the basic shirt and padded arming cap worn under the armour can be seen.

COATS-OF-PLATE

In the 14th century, the lower layers of clothing and armour were similar to those worn earlier, but the knight had extra protection on his arms, elbows, legs, knees and feet. The strongest item of armour was now the coat-of-plates, made of metal scales and plate covered in decorative cloth. Finally, a knight's lady might also give him a 'favour' to wear on his helmet during a tournament; perhaps a piece of coloured cloth or even an item of clothing!

14th CENTURY KNIGHTS

10 Coat-of-plates	15 Coif over arming cap
11 Surcoat	16 Padded arming cap
12 Arm plates	
13 Leg plates	17 Shirt
14 Helmet	18 Lance

Armourers were among the most skilled and highly paid craftsmen in the Middle Ages. They formed some of the first guilds, which were a bit like trade unions. They made arms and armour that not only protected the knight, but was often also very beautiful.

Many medieval manuscripts show knights charging at a piece of equipment called a quintain. Just how it really helped train a knight remains a bit of a mystery!

I n the early days making, or 'dubbing', a knight meant that a military leader gave his knights the arms, armour and horses that they needed to carry out their duties. But by the 13th century dubbing had become an elaborate ceremony, usually with a strong religious feel.

SQUIRES

In the 12th and 13th centuries knighthood was basically a military way of life. Being dubbed did not mean a man's military status or position in society was fixed, or that his descendants would be knights in future generations. If a soldier did not have the necessary equipment or was not wealthy enough to afford it, he simply could not be a knight.

The first step to becoming a knight was to become a squire. Squires might be the sons of other knights, or the sons of nobles. Starting at about the age of ten, they had to learn all the skills of knighthood. These included how to use and care for weapons, how to ride and look after a horse, and how to fight alongside other knights as part of a team.

ELABORATE CEREMONIES

When a squire had learned these skills, he could become a knight. His lord gave him land to live on. In return he promised to defend his lands and the Church, and to fight in his lord's army.

By the 14th century the ceremony promoting a squire to the rank of knight could be long and elaborate. If a young squire was from an important family, he would probably have to pray alone all night in church, wearing special clothes to show how humble he was before God. Then there was a splendid religious ceremony followed by an even more magnificent feast. More often, several squires would go through simpler versions of these ceremonies as a group.

In the 12th century, a knighting, or dubbing, ceremony could be carried out in camp before a battle or a siege. In this simple and old-fashioned form of dubbing, the Church played a minor role, perhaps with a monk simply blessing the men and their weapons.

Hunting in the forests around a castle formed an essential part of a knight's military training. It polished his riding skills and trained him to use cover, understand the layout of the land and to co-operate with other huntsmen. Some types of hunting involved the same weapons used in battle.

THE CHURCH'S ROLE

The Church had not always been involved in the dubbing ceremony. Once the Vikings and other threats had been defeated, the knights of western Europe found that they now had a

lot of military power. The result was chaos in many parts of Europe as knights fought for kings, barons, or simply for their own profit.

During the 11th and 12th centuries the Christian Church tried to control these troublesome soldiers. If they became 'Christian warriors', they were offered a chance of a place in Heaven in return. Not only could the knights join the ruling class, but they could also save their souls. To increase their influence over the knights, the Church began to play a bigger role in the dubbing ceremony. Swords, once blessed to bring luck or ward off evil, were now seen as versions of the Christian cross.

THE BATTLING KNIGHT

The Church and the knights were not always allies. After all, a knight's job meant using violence, even though his sword should only be used against enemies of the Church. If there was an emergency, a military leader could use the old system and dub as many squires as he could afford to equip, with virtually no ceremony at all. He could even dub merchants and craftsmen from the towns if he needed more men in a hurry.

The training of knights, and young squires who had not yet reached the status of knight, concentrated on strength, fitness, individual skill with weapons, and above all the ability to fight as part of a team of disciplined armoured horsemen.

Medieval horsemen used spurs to prick the sides of their horses when they wanted the animals to go faster. Gilded or decorated spurs became the most important badge of knightly rank. This late 14th-century example has a revolving spiked disc at the back.

11

THE FEUDAL SYSTEM

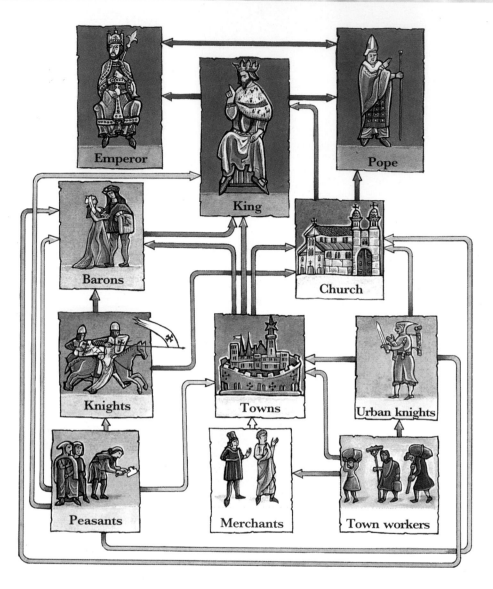

Emperor

King

Pope

Barons

Church

Knights

Towns

Urban knights

Peasants

Merchants

Town workers

This diagram shows how the Feudal System was supposed to work. Each arrow shows the loyalty or service owed by one group of people to their feudal superiors. For example, knights were usually given estates by a baron or the Church and so owed loyalty to them. Even here the pattern is greatly simplified!

Once a knight was accepted as a member of the aristocracy, he had to take on new duties. In fact the knight became the most important element in what is called the Feudal System. He defended the peasants while they worked to feed him and the rest of society.

At least, that was the theory. In fact there never was one version of the Feudal System. It varied from place to place, as well as from century to century. Some historians even say that the Feudal System never really existed!

THE FEUDAL SYSTEM

The most typical Feudal System in the 12th and 13th centuries was found in the country. There was a king at the top and peasants at the bottom, with knights somewhere in the middle.

A knight usually lived in a castle or manor house on an estate, called a fief, pronounced 'fee'. This was a piece of land where the peasants produced enough food and taxes to support the knight and his household. He gathered taxes, took his turn to guard a castle for the local baron, and might serve in his lord's army. Barons, in turn, governed large areas in the king's name – though they were often as powerful as the king himself.

PROBLEMS WITH THE SYSTEM

However, in many parts of Europe there was not enough land for all knights to have fiefs. Many were given money fiefs. These might be taxes on trade or tolls on a market or road. In some places, knights lived in towns (see page 42). Thus a knight might also feel loyalty to the town and its merchants, as well as the person who had given him the money fief.

A knight promised to be loyal to his lord or king in a special ceremony, and to do military service for him. In return the lord or king promised to protect the knight and usually gave him a fief to live on.

THE CHURCH

Many knights lived on lands owned by the Church. The Church and its bishops often felt that their first loyalty was to the Pope and to God, not to a king. Some other knights simply served as paid mercenaries for whoever offered the most money (see page 43), which meant that they were outside the Feudal System altogether. This led to more confusion and divided loyalties.

During the 11th century the Church needed the support of law-abiding knights to impose the Peace of God. Below, knights help a priest arrest a knight, or robber-baron, who has been breaking the law. Only knights had the military power to stop other knights ignoring the law.

THE PEACE OF GOD

As a result, many powerful barons and knights believed that they were free to fight their own private wars. This brought chaos and fear to places such as southern France and Germany. Most of the kings were too weak to stop these wars. The Church tried to bring back law and order through the Peace of God movement. This insisted that private wars could only be fought on certain days of the week. Rulers also tried to impose rules dealing with who could fight and who could be attacked. Gradually, some order was restored, but some kings, barons and knights continued to fight each other.

Knights did not only fight as heavily armoured cavalry in battle. They also had to guard and defend castles, and command the sergeants and militias (local soldiers) in fortified towns. In return, local men, women and children had their own duties, such as bringing food and water for the soldiers.

HORSES AND TACTICS

Destriers, specially bred war-horses, were very expensive so they were looked after carefully. Books were written on the subject. Some of them included advanced veterinary science translated from Arabic (see page 35).

The knight's most important possession was his specially bred war-horse, the 'destrier'. Without this expensive animal, the knight could not be a full member of the cavalry elite. In training he practised using weapons while riding this large animal, and fighting in a close-packed, highly disciplined cavalry formation. These horses were more like modern horses used in show-jumping and cross-country than lumbering carthorses, and they were looked after very carefully.

THE KNIGHT AND HIS HORSE

In battle, a closely packed group of knights on horseback walked into the attack, then lowered their lances to make their final charge at a slow canter. The sight of a dozen knights riding side by side, with the blades of their lances only a metre apart, must have been a frightening one.

When charging, a knight almost stood in his stirrups (foot supports), gripped around his hips by the raised back of his tall, wood-framed saddle. He held his heavy lance, about four metres long, in the 'couched' position, locked tight under the right armpit. This meant it could only be moved a little to the left or right so he could aim carefully at his target, but gave him a very firm grip on the lance. Basically, the knight, horse and lance became an almost unstoppable 'missile'. It was very difficult for another knight, let alone a soldier on foot, to knock a knight off his horse. But if unhorsed, it was quite difficult for him to get back on again.

Based on the early 14th-century English Luttrell Psalter, this picture shows Sir Geoffrey Luttrell and his war-horse, fully armoured and with the Luttrell coat-of-arms (see pages 18-19) displayed on their equipment. Sir Geoffrey is being given his helmet and shield by his wife and daughter. Their clothes show their own heraldry.

14

THE ARMY

Knights were the leaders and backbone of most western European armies. They were supported by the squires, who only fought in an emergency, and professional cavalry sergeants who were not members of the aristocracy. There were also professional infantry sergeants, including highly paid crossbowmen. The thousands of ordinary foot soldiers might include well-equipped men from towns, or peasants forced to leave their homes in the country, who were often almost useless in battle.

By the 12th and 13th century Italian knights fought on foot more often than French and German knights. They also had some of the most advanced arms and armour. The Italian knights in this carving have coats-of-arms displayed on their helmets, shields and their horses' cloth coats.

BATTLE TACTICS

To win a battle, the knights of one army usually had to defeat the knights of the enemy army. The other soldiers tried to protect their own knights. One of the most important battle tactics was the conrois. This was a close formation of knights designed to charge at standing infantry or other cavalry, and was the 'tank' of medieval warfare. Only a brave and disciplined enemy could resist a conrois of fully armoured knights if it did hit its target.

However, unlike a modern tank, the conrois could only 'shoot forwards'. If it was attacked from the side or rear it was almost helpless. It was also difficult to turn or stop a conrois once it had started to charge, and it was even more difficult to bring the knights back together if they got split up. In fact the conrois had to deliver a knock-out blow – or its knights could soon be defeated.

THE BATTLE OF MARCHFELD

The Battle of Marchfeld in AD 1278 (shown below) was a typical clash between armoured cavalry knights. The Bohemian knights fought their enemy, the Austrian and Hungarian knights, to a standstill. However, a force of Turkish horse-archers who were fighting with the Austrians were nimble enough to get around the right side of the Bohemian conrois formations. Shooting arrows from horseback, they caused havoc. With their knights defeated, the Bohemians lost the battle.

On the battlefield, powerful infantry crossbows and field fortifications, such as rows of sharp stakes, could stop an advancing 'conrois'. These tactics enabled the armies of small Italian states (left) to defeat the knights of larger German forces (right).

Key for Battle of Marchfeld

Bohemian camp

Turkish horse-archers from the Hungarian army

Austrians

Hungarians

Bohemians

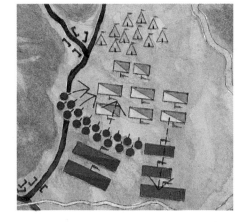

MEDIEVAL CASTLES

The castle of Eltz is a typical example of the kind of hill-top fortification built in Germany. It is called a 'randhausburgen', which means 'surrounding-house-castle'. Sited on a natural outcrop of rock, it was difficult to attack.

Castles were the homes of kings, barons and their knights, as well as servants and other staff. Castles were also centres of local government as well as local defence. From them, law and order was maintained in the surrounding countryside.

MAGNIFICENCE AND SQUALOR

Castles looked very important, but they were uncomfortable to live in. There was little privacy for anyone, except for the lord and his lady, who had their own bedroom. Meals were eaten together, there were only basic washing facilities and toilets were almost as public as meals! Despite the dirt and noise, life in a castle had a certain magnificence and can rarely have been boring.

LIFE IN THE CASTLE

It was part of a baron or knight's duty to behave in a grand manner, entertain guests and give work to other knights, servants and labourers. Knights, squires, and sergeants of the castle would train in the courtyard, while armourers would be repairing weapons in the outbuildings. Food would be grown, taxes collected, and hunts organized for military training and as an extra source of meat. If there was a war on, a strong guard would be mounted on the walls, while scouts scoured the countryside for information.

Gates were the weakest points in any castle. Different systems were developed to strengthen them, including several ways of raising and lowering a drawbridge. The illustration below left shows a drawbridge protected by an iron gate called a portcullis and raised by a winch. Below right is a drawbridge balanced by heavy counterweights.

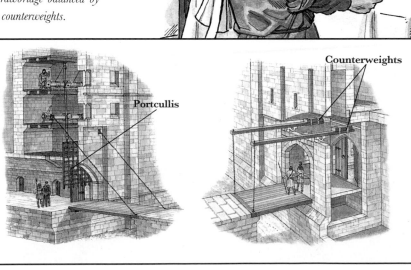

Counterweights

Portcullis

Feasts would be held in the castle's hall. They were very carefully organized, with many different courses of food and drink. The more important guests sat closest to the high table where the lord and lady sat.

UNDER SIEGE

Castles usually had to be captured by a siege. At the first sign of an attack, the defenders made sure the castle had enough food, water, wine and military supplies to last for months. They would also make sure the stores were filled with leather, nails and iron to repair weapons or armour. Any wooden buildings near the defences would be destroyed, so the enemy could not use the timber. The castle's commander would also send messages to his lord asking for help.

ATTACK

The defenders might also attack the enemy before they had time to set up camp. If this failed, the defenders would retreat inside their fortifications. From there they would make sorties (attacks) to try to destroy the attackers' siege machines and food supplies.

HONOURABLE SURRENDER

If this failed, a castle's commander would often agree to surrender if help had not arrived by an agreed date. In return, the attackers would agree not to harm the castle's defenders when they surrendered. They might even let the defenders keep their weapons if they promised not to fight in the rest of the war. However, defenders got little mercy if they had refused to surrender when given the chance.

Only in the most desperate situation would attackers try to take a castle by storm, because too many soldiers would be killed. Instead, they would wait for the castle to run out of food, or batter down the walls with siege engines.

This manuscript shows the siege of Savona in Italy in 1227. Attackers and defenders both have stone-throwing 'mangonels'. These were basically enormous slings on beams powered by men and women pulling on ropes. Each side is trying to destroy the other's artillery. In the 12th century the counterweight mangonel, or 'trebuchet', was invented in the Middle East. This used heavy weights instead of people pulling ropes.

Warriors have painted designs on their shields and armour since ancient times. What made medieval heraldry special was that the designs used in 'coats-of-arms' were handed down from generation to generation. They could be used to show which family or political group a knight belonged to. A knight who had designs painted on his shield, helmet, or woven into his clothes could be identified easily.

Direct relation ——————→
Political claim —·—·—·→
Political allegiance ·········→

This 'pommel' from the grip of a sword has the coat-of-arms of Dreux on one side and a typical French Crusader's cross on the other. It was found in Damascus (now Syria) and was almost certainly lost by Peter of Dreux, Count of Brittany, when he was captured by Egyptian Mamluks in AD 1250.

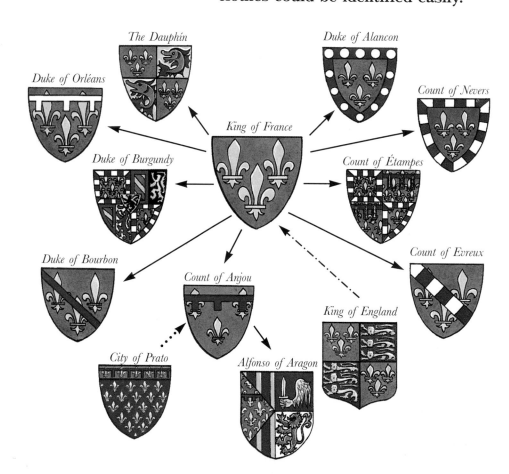

The relationships between different parts of the French Royal Family were shown in a pictorial way by heraldry. Marriage alliances and even political loyalty to France by foreigners could also be shown.

'Each strives to arm himself
with a new clean surcoat.
One has a tower shining
brightly on his shield,
One a lion, one a boar...
This man bears a black banner,
another white, another blue...
another blazoned with
a red coat covered with leaves.'

— From the poem 'Galeran' —

WHY HERALDRY?

One reason heraldry appeared was because helmets had wider face-protectors at the front, and mail hoods called 'coifs' (page 8). These covered most of the face so that knights could not be recognized. Heraldry became a way of identifying a knight in armour on the battlefield.

A SPECIAL CODE

Some of the knights who fought in the Crusades (see pages 28-29) may have seen designs used by Arab and Byzantine soldiers. The Crusaders brought home the idea, and began using heraldry as a special code. The code allowed a knight's family background and political connections to be 'read' by anyone who knew the language of heraldry.

In the 12th and 13th centuries, a passion for new warlike sports called 'tournaments' swept through Europe (see pages 22-23). At first these involved teams of horsemen and sometimes infantry in mock battles. Heraldic shields and clothes became essential 'team colours' for the spectators and for each side to tell from a distance which team was which.

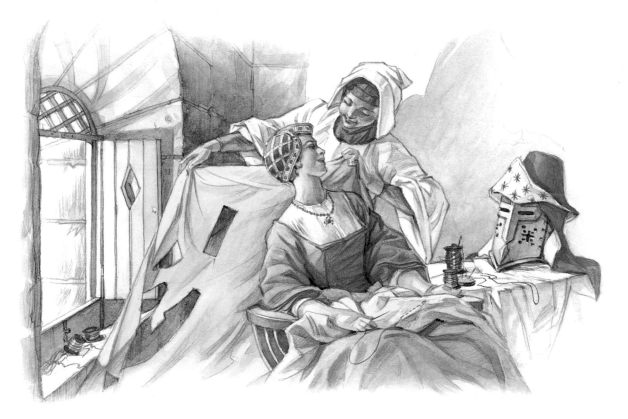

FAMILY COATS-OF-ARMS

By the end of the 12th century the basic rules of heraldry had developed. A fixed set of colours and a basic pattern were used by each noble family. This coat-of-arms was then inherited by a man's eldest son. His younger sons would make theirs slightly different to the original, and their sons would add even more differences. Sometimes, husbands would add their wives' coat-of-arms to their own in a system called quartering, particularly if they had married into a powerful family.

Heraldry not only identified troops on the battlefield, but was also used to describe events in manuscripts. In the Italian chronicle below, the city state of Florence is asking for help from the King of France. The city can be recognized because, like the blue and gold French banner (also on page 18), the Florentine flag includes a fleurs-de-lys.

BADGES OF LOYALTY

Merchant families that had risen to the knightly class took pride in this fact by including something to do with their trade, such as business or farming, on their coats-of-arms. Towns did the same. For example, seaports included ships, while towns used crossed keys to show that their loyalty was – or had been – to the Pope.

In some parts of Europe, small states would also show their loyalty to a more powerful kingdom by adding part of its coat-of-arms to their own. In Italy, the little city of Prato and the powerful city of Florence used the French fleurs-de-lys to show loyalty to France (page 18).

One of the main reasons for the use of heraldry was the development of new forms of helmet that completely hid a knight's face so that he could not be recognized by friends or followers. This 13th-century bronze container called an 'aquamanile' shows a knight wearing an early form of 'Great Helm'. The aquamanile could have held water or wine during a banquet.

Like all forms of hunting, falconry was used to get meat for eating. It was also a very aristocratic sport and was often associated with romantic flirting between men and women.

As knights changed from hard-bitten soldiers into members of the wealthy aristocracy, they started to take an interest in the finer things of life. By the 12th century they were enjoying music, reading, colourful clothes and exotic food from foreign lands. They also started to treat women *almost* as equals! It was the dawn of the age of Courtly Love.

TREATMENT OF WOMEN

In medieval Europe, the idea that men should treat women not as possessions or producers of healthy sons, would have sounded crazy. Then came a shocking foreign fashion for admiring ladies from a distance and doing heroic deeds just to win a smile. Like many new ideas, this one originally came from the Muslim Arab world: Crusaders returning from the Middle East began to behave in a much more civilized way than before!

COURTLY LOVE

Knights and squires were now encouraged to worship a beautiful woman and do heroic deeds in her name. She in turn would flirt with him and praise his bravery as far as was considered proper. This horrified the Church. Not only did the new fashion come from non-Christian lands, but the Church feared it might turn the knights into 'softies'.

CHIVALRY

However, the idea of Courtly Love soon became part of the ceremonies and customs of knighthood, in a code of conduct called chivalry. As well as fighting for his lord and protecting the Church, a chivalrous knight was now expected to be polite to women, to defend the weak, and to be truthful and honorable.

Minstrels and music sometimes played a part in the dubbing ceremony (page 10). The young Francis of Assisi is given the sword and spurs that mark his promotion to the status of knight, while minstrels play a form of lute and doubled flute.

LADIES AND MINSTRELS

The idea of Courtly Love was spread by travelling singers called 'minstrels'. They sang new love songs played on unusual musical instruments from the Middle East.

The songs were so popular that even the Church grudgingly changed its opinion, especially when some of the best songs were being written by monks and nuns.

NEW INSTRUMENTS

The minstrels of the 12th to 14th centuries had different names in other countries, but they all sang similar songs. In northern France they were called 'troubadours' and in Germany 'minnesingers'.

Their music changed over the years. At first it was played on simple instruments, like flutes and drums. Then travellers brought new ones from the East, such as the lute (similar to an Arabic instrument called an oud), or the viol (which was played with a bow and seems to have been brought from China by the Turks).

AN INTEREST IN ART

Quite suddenly it seemed that an almost barbaric western Europe was becoming interested in things other than warfare. In more peaceful areas, like England, many knightly families moved from being full-time warriors to being country gentlemen. They took more interest in the well-being of their peasants, and in agriculture and business, than in military training. In places like France, Germany and Italy, some knights and squires won fame as troubadours.

PATRONS

Once the ideals of Courtly Love had caught on, they encouraged an interest in art. The wealthier knights and nobles became patrons. Instead of using their wealth to build castles and fight wars, they began to pay artists, writers, poets, craftspeople and academics to work for them. Many great religious works of art were paid for by knights and nobles.

The lute became a favourite instrument with minstrels. Its name comes from the Arabic 'al-oud' which simply meant 'the oud'.

The older generation often seem to think that the young are lazy or too busy enjoying themselves. This was certainly the case in the early 12th century. As the knightly class got richer and life became more comfortable, young squires were often criticized for spending too much time on the latest troubadour songs, and for not working hard enough at their military training.

THE TOURNAMENT

Medieval tournaments were originally a form of military training for cavalrymen. They helped a knight refresh the skills needed to control a horse and the use of his weapons. Tournaments became the most popular spectator sport of the Middle Ages. Some knights travelled all over Europe to display their skills. However, by the 15th century these splendid, expensive events had almost nothing to do with real warfare. They were a way of winning fame and fortune, because winners often took the loser's horse or even his armour.

The training of Charlemagne's milites or cavalrymen was basically the same as that of the Roman cavalry. It involved teams taking turns to throw blunt javelins at each other, the other side defending themselves with their shields.

ORIGINS OF THE TOURNAMENT

When Charlemagne and his successors built up their armies in the 8th and 9th centuries, they used some complicated forms of training based on the methods of the old Roman and Persian armies. For example, teams of horsemen armed with javelins took turns to charge at each other. They would throw their blunted weapons, then turn away as a unit while the other team defended themselves with their shields.

By the 11th century, rival teams of knights were challenging each other, apparently just for fun. These matches gradually evolved into full-scale competitions, called tournaments, organized by leading kings and barons.

By the 15th century tournaments were an important spectator sport. The spectators the young knights really wanted to impress were young ladies, as this Italian wall painting of a joust makes very clear. The men on the ground are probably clearing up pieces of broken weapons.

MIXING IT IN THE MELÉE

The first sort of tournament was a mock battle that had more in common with real cavalry training. Two teams of knights, normally in close-packed conrois formations (see page 15), charged at each other. Then, when their formations had fallen apart, they mixed it in a general free-for-all called a melée. It was not as chaotic as it sounds, because there were judges who would disqualify a knight for making an unfair blow, or would try to separate the teams if things got out of hand. Some melées also involved units of foot soldiers who would try to help their own knights.

'During the skirmish a French squire from Beauce came forward alone and cried out, "Is there any gentleman among you who, for love of his lady, is willing to try a feat of arms with me? If there is one I am quite ready to ride forward, fully armed and mounted, to tilt three courses with the lance, to give three blows with the battle-axe, and three strokes with the dagger"... when his proposal was made known... an expert man at tournaments stepped forward and said, "I will accept his challenge; let him come out of the castle".'

—— From The Froissart Chronicles ——

JOUSTING

Jousting, in which two individual horsemen charged at each other, probably began as a way of settling disputes, letting off steam or simply warming up. It only became popular in the 13th century. Not only was jousting more entertaining for the audience who could cheer on their own favourite, also it allowed a knight to show off his own bravery and skill (see front cover and pages 46–47).

All forms of tournament were very dangerous. As many knights seem to have been killed in tournaments as died in battle (though of course there were many more tournaments than real battles). Later, rules were introduced to make them safer. For example, a knight had to hit his opponent's shield or helmet; hitting his legs or horse was counted as a foul.

A COLOURFUL SPORT

By the 15th century tournaments were hardly more dangerous than modern sports, though a lot more colourful. Nevertheless, knights could still challenge opponents to a dangerous fight with real war-weapons rather than with blunt blades.

Images of the tournament were often used to illustrate romantic stories. Here knights are not fighting each other but are besieging a 'Castle of Love' which is guarded by ladies who defend themselves by throwing flowers at the 'enemy'.

In this Italian wall-painting, Geoffrey de Bouillon, the first ruler of the Kingdom of Jerusalem, is armed for tournament combat on foot – in the style of the late 15th century. The female figure is carrying a kind of pickaxe used in duels to settle legal arguments.

A MANOR HOUSE

The outbuildings of the manor house were full of activity, including cider making. The inset, far right, shows a special barrel-shaped cider-press. This crushes the apples, then the juice is strained through a cloth before being put in barrels to brew. The only brick or stone structure in many manor houses was the chimney; the rest was made of timber and plaster. Even with a roaring fire the lord and lady's chamber (shown when the see-through scene is turned) was probably chilly. But it was still more comfortable than a castle!

As early as the 13th century, many English knights were turning away from their old warlike way of life to something a lot more peaceful. Compared with most other parts of Europe, England at this time was a peaceful place. As a result, the knightly class gradually changed from professional soldiers to 'village squires', the leaders of society in the rural areas. They were more concerned with the well-being of their peasants, selling the wool from their sheep and keeping local law-and-order, than fighting the king's enemies in foreign lands.

THE PEACEFUL KNIGHT

By the late 14th century most English knights and their families lived in comfortable manor houses rather than cold and draughty castles. Of course, the manor houses had to be defended, since even England had outlaws, pirates, political disturbances, uprisings in Wales and invasions by the Scots or French.

The manor house shown below is based on some buildings and deserted moats that can still be seen in the English countryside. The defences consist of a wooden stockade and drawbridge. Inside this stockade is the main house and some outbuildings consisting of stables and a brewery where servants are making cider.

EVERYDAY LIFE

Much of the everyday life and work of the manor house takes place in the open air, in the courtyard. In the scene below, boys on a wheeled wooden hobby-horse are tilting at a quintain, while young men are practising sword-play. There are some armourers mending weapons and shields, perhaps because there are problems with outlaws. Meanwhile, some peasants are taking a cart loaded with cider to sell at the local market.

INSIDE THE HOUSE

Inside the main house, the knight's family dine in the main hall. The other downstairs rooms are used for storage and work, including the kitchen and the buttery for storing barrels of wine, beer or salted food. Only the lord of the manor and his close family have any privacy. At night they will sleep in the only bedroom on the first floor. But as it is now daytime, this is where women spin, bathe the children and carry out other household chores.

THE VILLAGE

Beyond the moat is a small chapel. Also close to the manor house is a village. The villagers look to the knight and his family for protection, and also for advice.

When you turn the see-through scene, can you see the smoke from a distant warning beacon? This is a signal for the local forces to assemble, led by the local knight. The knight's duties also included keeping law-and-order in the surrounding villages, and serving as a link with the king's government.

1 **Chapel**
2 **Moat**
3 **Drawbridge**
4 **Stockade**
5 **Stable**
6 **Brewery**
7 **Great hall**
8 **Kitchen**
9 **Lord and lady's bedroom**

Knights usually wanted to appear in armour on their tombs, even if they were really peaceful country gentlemen. The incised brass carving, above, marked the tomb of Sir John de la Pole and his wife. Sir John is shown in full armour of the late 14th century.

PILGRIMAGE

Pilgrim routes criss-crossed Europe and the Mediterranean. The most important centres of pilgrimage were Jerusalem, Rome, Santiago de Compostela in Spain, and Canterbury. Other important centres of pilgrimage mostly attracted local visitors.

Most medieval people were deeply religious. They believed that penance (something you do to show you are sorry for your sins), or making some sort of sacrifice, could wash their sins away and save their souls from Hell. One of the most important forms of penance was to go on pilgrimage (visit a holy place).

SAVING THE SOUL

Pilgrimage to Christian sites was extremely important during the Middle Ages. Poor people, including lower-ranking knights, visited the tombs of local saints since only the rich could travel very far. To reach one of the most important Christian centres, such as Rome or Jerusalem, cost a lot of money. If the pilgrim was not rich, they would only be able to go as part of the staff of a great lord.

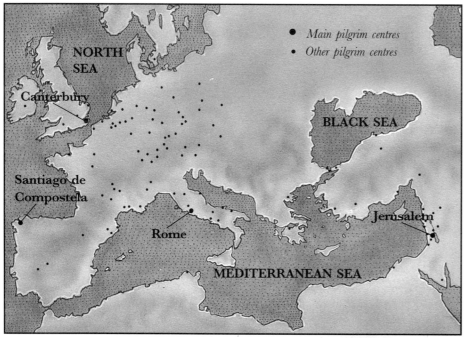

- Main pilgrim centres
- Other pilgrim centres

NORTH SEA

Canterbury

BLACK SEA

Santiago de Compostela

Rome

Jerusalem

MEDITERRANEAN SEA

Going on pilgrimage was a hazardous undertaking. The main dangers were disease, shipwreck and attack by robbers. Even in peacetime groups of pilgrims might need a knight to travel with them for protection. In the Holy Land this would probably be a Hospitaller or Knight Templer (see pages 36–37).

Almost every country in Christendom had its own pilgrimage centres, but the most important of all was the Holy Sepulchre in Jerusalem. Christian pilgrims made their way there before the Crusades, and they continued to do so after the Crusader Kingdom of Jerusalem had been destroyed.

DANGER ON THE ROAD

Travelling was also hard and dangerous. Many people were attacked by bandits and outlaws. Roads were bad, there were no hotels, and inns were very basic. Instead, people tried to rest at monasteries, or at one of the special hostels run for pilgrims by monks or friars along the main pilgrim routes.

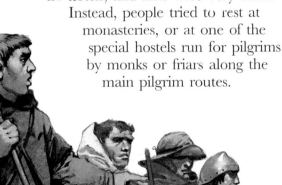

KNIGHTS ON PILGRIMAGE

The Church encouraged knights to go on pilgrimage so they could protect other pilgrims from bandits and outlaws. The knights and their families responded enthusiastically, because they were often adventurous by nature. Perhaps knights also believed their souls needed saving because their job involved such violence and bloodshed.

RELIGIOUS TOURISM

However, as travelling conditions improved during the late Middle Ages, knights, merchants, rich peasants and a number of strong-minded women went on pilgrimage just for the fun of it. Many were more like modern tourists than the serious pilgrims of earlier centuries. They even collected 'souvenirs', lead badges with the symbols of the saint or religious event linked with the place they had visited.

Those who wanted real adventure now had to go further afield to the Holy Land in the Middle East, which had been reconquered by the Muslims. Knights who had very guilty consciences could either give up all their worldly goods and family to join one of the Military Orders (see pages 36-37) or volunteer to fight alongside the Orders for just one season.

One of the most popular pilgrim badges in England was 'Thomas Becket's Flask'. This miniature lead container was supposed to contain the saint's diluted blood, which was believed to work miraculous cures on the sick.

Not all centres of pilgrimage were simply religious. Some were famous because they contained the tombs of great rulers, such as Charlemagne, who was regarded almost as a saint in the Middle Ages. This golden reliquary, containing his bones, portrayed him as Sanctus Karolus Imperator, builder of a new and Christian Roman Empire, a man blessed by God and supported by the Church.

The Byzantine Empire was the eastern half of the old Roman Empire. In the late 11th century, the Seljuk Turks overran half of the Byzantine Empire. In desperation the Emperor begged for help from the West. He wanted trained mercenaries to join his armies in Constantinople – instead he got a Crusade!

DEUS VULT – 'IT IS GOD'S WILL!'

The First Crusade to reconquer the Holy Land was called by Pope Urban II in 1095. Although Jerusalem had been ruled by Muslims for over 400 years, the Seljuk Turks had been making it difficult for pilgrims to visit the Holy Land. The Crusade was sent to uphold the Christian religion against the Islamic religion.

The Pope probably did not expect his call to take back Jerusalem to be so popular. In 1096 over 5,000 knights, many from France, 'took the cross' and marched east with 'Deus Vult – It is God's Will' as their battlecry. Thousands of ordinary people did the same. About 150,000 men, women and children became 'Crusaders'.

Western European warriors were recruited by the Byzantine Empire long before the Crusades. They included Normans, as well as Anglo-Saxons who had fled from England after the Norman Conquest – so quarrels were probably quite common.

The citadel of Amasya in Turkey includes a great deal of medieval Byzantine fortification. The tower, shaped like the prow of a ship, on the left is typically Byzantine. The citadel was an important military base used to defeat a Christian Crusade in AD 1101.

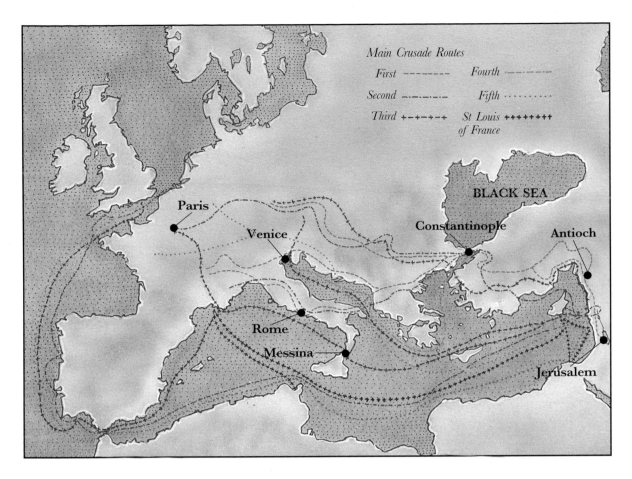

Main Crusade Routes

First --------- Fourth -------

Second ----- Fifth ··········

Third +-+-+-+ St Louis +++++++
of France

BLACK SEA

Paris

Venice

Constantinople

Antioch

Rome

Messina

Jerusalem

THE CAPTURE OF JERUSALEM

The Middle Eastern Crusades are seen as important events in European history since they were heroic efforts to save the Holy Land from Muslim rule. In fact, the First Crusade was the only successful one. It conquered Palestine, most of Lebanon, part of Jordan and part of Syria. In 1099, a force of just 1,000 knights and 10,000 other soldiers managed to capture Jerusalem, and set up a number of Crusader states.

Like later Crusades, the First Crusade was marked by great cruelty and suffering. Few of the knights knew anything about the land and its difficult climate, and many were killed by thirst, hunger and disease rather than by their enemies. The Crusaders also killed thousands of Muslims when they captured Jerusalem (see page 30).

LATER CRUSADES

Later Crusades involved knights and other professional soldiers rather than ordinary people. They were generally better organized and equipped than the First Crusade, and for almost 200 years they managed to defend part of what had already been won.

WHY THE CRUSADES FAILED

However, Crusades that tried to take more land almost always failed, despite involving some of the very best armies of knights that Europe could gather. Such disasters puzzled the knights and churchmen. The churchmen were convinced God was on their side and the knights were sure they were the best fighting men in the world. In fact the success of the First Crusade had been a fluke, because it had hit the Muslim Middle East at a time of great weakness. Once the Muslim armies got over the first shock, they quickly learned how to deal with the Crusaders' tactics.

THE THIRD CRUSADE

By the time the Third Crusade reached the Holy Land, Richard the Lionheart of England, Philip of France and Frederick Barbarossa of Germany found themselves up against the great Saracen ruler, Saladin, who was now in control of Jerusalem. The knights, sergeants and other troops of England, France and the German Empire did their best but could not even reach Jerusalem, let alone retake it from Saladin's soldiers.

Experience fighting the Muslims, Mongols and Byzantines taught western knights a great deal and encouraged the development of new forms of arms and armour. The so-called 'dog-face bascinet' with its mail neck protection, below, is an example of how European armourers learned from the East and then added their own ideas.

FIGHTING FOR THE CROSS

The success of the First Crusade was never repeated. This late 13th-century manuscript shows the Crusaders' desperate but eventually successful attack on the city of Antioch.

Most of the Crusades to the Holy Land failed, though the Crusaders did hang on to some parts of the eastern Mediterranean coast until the late 13th century, as well as the island of Cyprus. The Fourth Crusade even attacked the Byzantine Empire and occupied Constantinople for more than 50 years!

CRUSADING AMID THE SNOWS

Other later Crusades tried to stop the Ottoman Turks destroying what was left of the Byzantine Empire and conquering the Balkans, part of central Europe and southern Russia. They failed as well. In fact, for the knights of western Europe the Crusades were a heroic disaster. In man-to-man combat with their enemies the heavily armoured knights were almost unbeatable. Yet tactically they were not as clever as the Muslims. The relatively small Crusader armies could never really hope to defeat Turkish and Arab forces who were defending their homes and land.

Far to the north, German knights led a series of Crusades against the pagan peoples of what are now northeast Germany, northern Poland and the Baltic states. They were much more successful. Here, knights, sergeants and warlike priests forced Christianity upon the natives at the point of a sword. These campaigns were very ruthless, and in the 14th century Lithuania, the last pagan state in Europe, finally accepted Christianity.

The First Crusade of 1096–1100 suffered terrible hardship as it marched across Europe and Turkey. Unused to the land and climate, many died from hunger, thirst and disease. When the Crusaders reached Jerusalem, many knights and ordinary soldiers went berserk, slaughtering not only Muslim soldiers but women and children.

SPAIN AND PORTUGAL

Things were also different in Spain and
Portugal. Here the Christians outnumbered
the Muslims and were much closer to their
own lands. The campaigns in Spain and
Portugal were known as the 'Reconquista'
rather than as Crusades, and they steadily
pushed the Christian frontier southwards,
from one chain of mountains, called
sierras, to the next. Eventually the Spanish
and Portuguese knights, helped by
volunteers from north of the Pyrenees,
retook Andalusia from the Muslims and
even tried to attack North Africa. The
greatest of the Spanish knights was
Rodrigo de Vivar, 'El Cid', meaning
'the master' in Arabic.

PEASANT CAVALRY

In most of Europe the armoured horsemen
were knights or squires, or at least
professional sergcants. In Spain they were
aided by ordinary villagers and townsmen
who formed large mounted militia forces.
These fought in almost exactly the same
way as their noble knightly neighbours.

*The Baltic Crusades are less
well known than those to the
Middle East. But they also had
their epic triumphs and disasters.
One of the most famous defeats
was on the frontier between
Estonia and Russia, in 1242.
On the frozen surface of Lake
Peipus, a force of Teutonic
Knights is said to have fallen
through the ice.*

*These two figures are from
a letter of loyalty sent by
the Italian town of Prato
to the King of Naples, who
was related to the Count of
Anjou (see page 18). The
well equipped soldier on the
left holds a shield that includes
the royal coat-of-arms. The
other knight's shield has the
Latin word 'LEX' (meaning
'law') to show that Prato's
loyalty was confirmed by law.*

THE SIEGE AT AIN HABIS

In 1182 the Muslim Saracen ruler of Damascus decided that the Crusader outpost in the cave-fortress of Ain Habis was too dangerous and had to be destroyed. So he sent some of his finest troops and famous miners who had already proved their worth in helping to seize other Crusader castles. This small force was so successful that the cave-fortress is said to have fallen after only five days.

The inset picture (right) shows Crusaders and Saracens battling it out in a mid-14th century European manuscript. The Muslims are pictured as unarmoured barbarians with cloths around their heads – in reality Arabs were often better equipped than their western foes!

The Crusaders, like their Saracen enemies, built some huge and complicated castles. They also used whatever they found when they needed a fortification in a hurry. These included ancient Roman theatres and temples, and caves in the mountains. One of the most famous cave fortresses was Ain Habis, or the 'Caves de Sueth'.

A CAVE FORTRESS

Long before the Crusaders arrived, one of the vertical cliffs overlooking the deep Yarmouk river valley was home to some Byzantine monks. Nobody knows when these monks left their isolated monastery.

A READY-MADE FORTRESS

The Crusaders did not have enough time, money or manpower to build a full-scale castle, so they took over the caves that the monks had cut into the cliff-face and linked by wooden walkways. From Ain Habis, the Crusaders could threaten the vital road that linked Damascus and other great cities of Syria with Arabia and Egypt.

Ain Habis might have had only a small garrison, but it was so important that the Saracens were determined to get it back.

1 **Muslim troops have broken through the stone gate**
2 **Old Byzantine monks' church**
3 **Saracen miners cut a steep passage to upper level**
4 **Wooden walkways joining sets of caves**
5 **Ladders between levels**
6 **Waterfall**
7 **Troughs channelling water into main cistern**
8 **Main water storage cistern**
9 **Crusader garrison defending upper caves and walkways**
10 **Upper living quarters including second church**

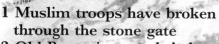

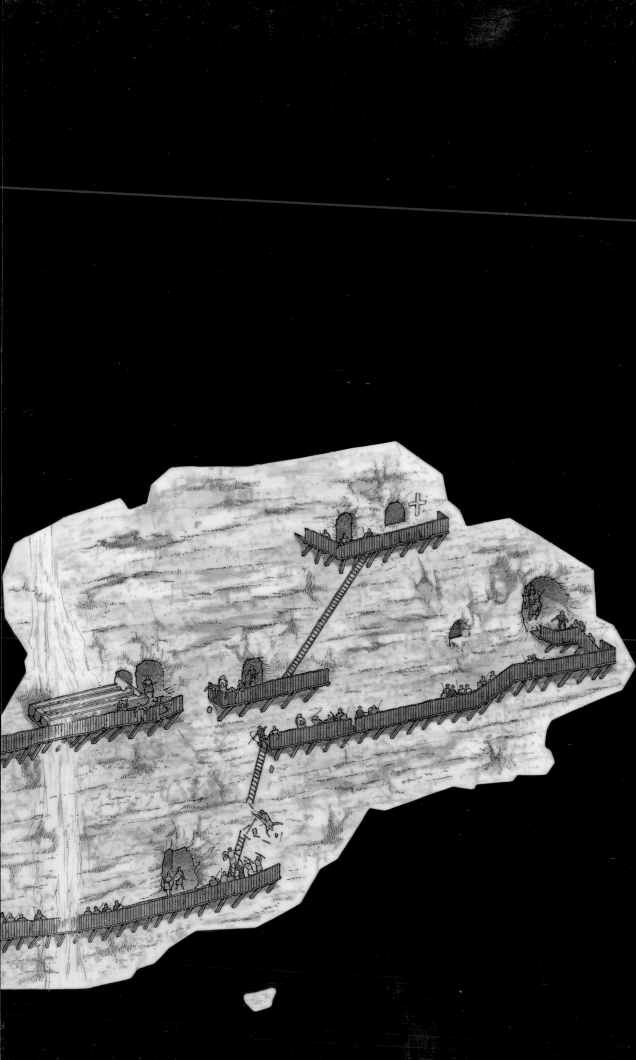

BATTLES FOR THE CAVES

But beseiging a series of caves in a cliff was not like attacking an ordinary castle. Their first assault, in 1158, was abandoned because the main Saracen army was defeated elsewhere. However, it convinced King Baldwin III of Jerusalem to send supplies and a bigger garrison to Ain Habis.

THE SARACENS SUCCEED

In 1182, the great Muslim ruler Saladin sent his nephew Farrukh Shah to attack again. This time the cave fortress fell after only five days. The attack is shown in the scene below, with Muslim miners digging a steep passage from next to a cave-church to one of the main store rooms above.

The Crusaders retook the caves that same year. Miners cut great boulders from the top of the cliff and sent them crashing onto the wooden walkways beneath, smashing the water troughs. The Muslim garrison could not survive without this.

'The Crusaders brought many stone-masons and put them on top of the mountains, placing a strong guard of horsemen and sergeants so they could work in safety day and night. They threw the rocks they excavated over the cliff (onto the defenders below).'

William of Tyre

WOUNDS AND MEDICINE

HORRORS OF WAR

Death from accidents or disease was so common that medieval people were probably more able to accept the sight of blood and the horrid reality of war. They also seemed capable of surviving terrible wounds, despite the basic medical facilities of the time. Perhaps if children and adults survived in the unhygienic world that surrounded them, they were more resistant to infection.

Descriptions of battles in medieval books say that the most common injuries were to the arms, legs and head. This was because a knight's body was largely protected by his armour and a shield. Studies of medieval battle skeletons have found this to be true.

The horrific injuries inflicted by medieval weapons were often illustrated in gruesome detail in medieval manuscripts. This scene from a 13th-century Bible shows Hebrews defeating the Amonnites.

Like soldiers in any period of history, knights faced the possibility of appalling injuries. Medieval weapons might look basic, but they could cut off an arm, leg or head with a single blow, while arrows sometimes really did fall like rain.

Because of the superiority of Islamic medical science, Muslim soldiers regarded the Crusaders as dirty and ignorant. It took a long time for European knights to accept that hot baths were good for you, rather than a luxury for soft Saracens. Baths were even found in Muslim military camps, shown below. They had earth walls roofed with palm leaves and hot water supplied from steaming cauldrons.

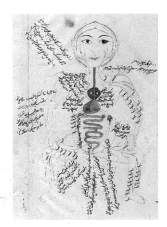

The horse (left) is being supported by a sling to keep its weight off an injured leg. Highly trained war-horses were extremely expensive and so knights were eager to learn about the advanced veterinary techniques used in Byzantium and the Muslim world.

Discovered in a mass grave from the Battle of Visby, 1361, the skull above was almost cut in half by a terrible blow across the front despite the fact that the wearer had a mail coif. Meanwhile Middle Eastern doctors had already discovered how the blood moved around the body (shown below), and how the eyes worked – information not believed in western Europe for centuries.

MEDICAL KNOWLEDGE

In the early Middle Ages, there were no doctors in the armies of western Europe. Instead priests did what they could, though this usually only meant giving words of comfort to the dying.

Ancient Greek medical knowledge had been forgotten in Europe, but was translated into Arabic by the Muslims. Arab and Persian doctors had discovered even more about how the body worked. By the 11th and 12th centuries the Crusaders had a chance to see just how their Muslim and Byzantine rivals were more advanced in the fields of medical and veterinary science.

MIDDLE EASTERN SUPERIORITY

For example, in the 12th century, a Saracen soldier, Usamah Ibn Munqidh, wrote about a European and an Arab doctor. A knight with an infected leg was brought to the Arab doctor who put a small poultice (medicated bandage) on it. The infection began to heal, but then the European doctor came along and said, 'This man knows nothing'. He turned to the knight and asked, 'What would you prefer, living with one leg or dying with

two?'. The knight replied, 'Living with one leg'. So the European doctor called for a strong soldier with a sharp axe. He put the knight's leg on a block of wood and told the soldier to cut it off with a single blow. This the soldier tried to do, but it needed two blows, at which point the patient died. The Arab doctor was not impressed; nor was Usamah.

LEARNING ON THE BATTLEFIELD

During the 13th and 14th centuries, the medical and veterinary knowledge of the Middle East was brought to Europe via the Crusaders and translated into Italian and Spanish. This meant that the science of medicine was again improving in many parts of Europe by the 15th century.

However, the Church was opposed to cutting up human bodies to study them, so a battle was a doctor's only chance to study the human body. Some doctors clearly knew what they were doing, because they also helped some people at the same time. For example, at the Battle of Fornovo in 1495, a wounded knight had several pieces of broken bone removed from his skull and was walking around the streets of Venice only a few weeks later.

KNIGHTS OF THE CROSS

No-one knows why the Crusading Military Orders suddenly appeared in Spain and the Holy Land during the 12th century. Some historians believe they were inspired by the 'ribats' where Muslims volunteered to pray and fight for their religion. Some Orders only lasted a short while; some still exist today, though as charitable organisations rather than armies of knights.

A SWORD FOR THE CHURCH

Knights who wanted to lead a religious life but found it difficult to give up fighting could join one of the Military Orders. Unlike monks who prayed for Christendom and stayed within the walls of their monasteries, members of a Military Order fought for the Church and could be sent anywhere in Christendom. They became known as Knights of the Cross.

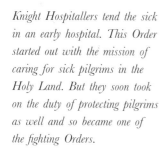

Knight Hospitallers tend the sick in an early hospital. This Order started out with the mission of caring for sick pilgrims in the Holy Land. But they soon took on the duty of protecting pilgrims as well and so became one of the fighting Orders.

Member of the Crusading Military Orders promised to give up all worldly possessions and, like monks, took a vow of poverty. For the Templers, the image of two knights riding a single horse reflects this poverty, though of course they did not really ride this way.

> '**I... do profess and promise chastity, giving up all property, and obedience to God and to the Blessed Virgin Mary and to you, Brother... Master of the Teutonic Order, and to your successors, according to the Rules and Regulations of the Order. And I will be obedient to you, and to your successors, even unto death.**'
>
> — *Brother-knights' Oath* —

MILITARY ORDERS

The most famous and successful of the Military Orders were the Templers, the Hospitallers and the Teutonic Knights, all of which were created in the 12th century. They became the shock troops of the Crusades and many other wars against non-Christians. In fact the Military Orders were so feared by their enemies that they were usually killed rather than taken prisoner. The cross of the Order was clearly visible on the clothes they wore.

BROTHER-KNIGHTS

Military Orders, such as the Templers, Hospitallers, Teutonic Knights and others, also attracted large numbers of ordinary knights who then became 'brother-knights'. Volunteers who were not knights served as sergeants or as non-military servants. Whatever their status, they gave up family, wealth and position in return for a hard and dangerous life, serving under very strict discipline and often in the most dangerous conditions.

Knights who did not want to dedicate themselves completely to the Military Orders became short-term members, serving in the Orders' armies for a year or even for just one campaign. They could then go home feeling they had fought for God, hopefully earned a place in heaven, and had also become heroes in the eyes of their friends.

The Templer church of Vera Cruz in Segovia, Spain. Many churches built for the Order of Templers were round, based on the Dome of the Rock in Jerusalem, which was thought to be the ancient temple where Jesus was shown to the priests. In fact it was a Muslim shrine built at the end of the 7th century.

A DANGEROUS LIFE

Brother-knights in the Crusader States, the Baltic or other warlike areas attacked their enemies, defended Christian territory against enemy raids, and kept up a tough daily training programme. They were supported by brother-knights based all over Europe who gathered money and supplies, and then sent them to the men on the front line. As a result the Military Orders soon became like powerful and rich international business corporations. They could even influence emperors and Popes.

MILITARY ORDERS AS RULERS

The Hospitallers and Teutonic Knights both ended up having their own states, the Hospitallers on the island of Rhodes and later on Malta, while the Teutonic Knights ruled much of what is now northern Poland, Latvia and Estonia.

The Templers, however, became so rich and powerful that the Pope and the King of France considered them a threat. The French king also hoped to take over their wealth. The Templer leadership was accused of spreading un-Christian beliefs. Confessions were forced out by torture and the leaders were executed. The Order's ordinary members were given lesser punishments or were dismissed. However, within months, the French king and the Pope were dead – just as one executed Templer leader had predicted!

Montfort in northern Palestine was the most important castle held by the German Military Order of Teutonic Knights in the Kingdom of Jerusalem. The Germans called it the Starkenberg which, like Montfort in French, means 'strong mountain'. Today it is in ruins, but the huge water cisterns that enabled its garrison to withstand a long siege still exist beneath the tumbled walls.

After the Crusades, the Knights Templers fought very few battles. In the 14th century, they were accused of not following the Christian faith and their leaders were tortured and then burned.

INVASION FROM THE EAST

This helmet of the Russian Prince Yaroslav Vsevolodovic (below) was found under a bush centuries after it was lost in battle. The silver icon (religious picture) on the front proclaimed that Yaroslav was a Christian ruler, and was also believed to give its wearer extra protection.

I**n the 13th century, a completely new enemy suddenly burst into eastern and central Europe – the Mongols. They seemed to appear from nowhere and they fought in a way that Russian warriors and European knights found almost impossible to deal with.**

THE MONGOLS

The Mongols were nomads from the plains to the east of Russia. They were tough warriors who rode fast horses and fought in the traditional Turkish manner as horse-archers. They had also learned a great deal from their Chinese enemies far to the east. A Mongol warrior could shoot his powerful bow from his saddle, and also carried a lance or sword. United under one ruthless ruler, the Great Khan Genghiz, their military discipline astonished the European knights.

Most fortifications in medieval Russia, along with almost all other buildings, were made of wood. The only stone buildings were a few important churches. This kind of timber and earth defence was very strong, but even so it could not withstand the Mongol onslaught.

This early 14th century manuscript from Iran shows the Mongols' different kinds of armour and powerful bows very accurately, along with the great war-drums they used as a way of communicating in battle.

THE MONGOLS ATTACK RUSSIA

First, the Mongols invaded Russia, taking their enemies completely by surprise. In winter their armies marched up the frozen rivers, using them as highways deep into the heart of Russia, so that the main cities fell within three years.

MONGOL VICTORY

Next, in 1241, the Mongols invaded central Europe. They astounded people with their ruthlessness and the speed at which their forces crossed great distances in almost all weathers. No wonder the knights of Europe called them 'The Devil's Horsemen'.

At the Battle of Liegnitz in Poland, the Mongols showered their enemies with arrows, then pretended to retreat. This lured the Teutonic Knights away from their army, so the Mongols could turn and crush them. Then, at the Sajo River, the Mongols used surprise attacks, smoke and noise to confuse a larger Hungarian army, which panicked and fled.

WHY DID THE MONGOLS STOP?

Suddenly the Mongols stopped their invasion of Europe, even though they had not been defeated. It seemed that they had just decided to go home. Many Christians believed this was 'Divine Intervention' (an act of God). In fact, the Great Khan had died, so his generals had gone to Mongolia to choose a successor and protect themselves against rivals.

The Mongols never returned to continue their invasion because they were not interested in taking over what they considered to be a relatively poor and backward part of the world – Europe!

The Mongols were successful partly because they were willing to recruit soldiers from people they had conquered. This early 14th-century illustration shows Mongol troops, including a Middle Eastern Muslim Arab (obviously a specialist) operating a stone-throwing 'trebuchet'.

The Mongol horse-archers appeared indestructible, faster and more mobile than western European knights. They also used fearsome new Chinese weapons – including early forms of gunpowder.

KNIGHTS AFLOAT

Many medieval ports were surrounded by defensive walls, with towers overlooking their narrow entrance. The entrance could be blocked by a floating boom or a chain raised and lowered with a winch, shown on the right hand page. The tower would have contained a small mangonel similar to the one shown top right. Within the safety of this inner harbour ships were built, repaired, loaded and unloaded. When the see-through page is turned, we can see the left-hand tarida being loaded with the knights' horses and armour ready for battle, while the right-hand merchant ship holds knights and supplies.

In some parts of medieval Europe, knights were as likely to find themselves serving aboard ship as in an army on land. Knights used lighter armour and weapons aboard ship than when riding a war-horse.

THE KNIGHT AS MARINE

The Italian merchant states of Venice and Genoa were the most powerful naval powers of the Middle Ages. Their knights played the part of marines defending merchant ships and war-galleys. Rivals joked that Venetian knights had webbed feet and did not know how to ride properly! This was just jealousy: northern Italian armies often defeated large and powerful German and French armies. At sea, the knights and their crossbowmen were able to defeat anyone that got in their way.

MEDIEVAL FIGHTING SHIPS

The main medieval fighting ship was the galley. This used sails when cruising peacefully and relied on oars during battle. The oarsmen were not slaves, but free men paid by the shipowners. The ship's 'sailors' were a small and highly skilled group of men who handled the sails.

THE TARIDA

This was a specialized galley invented by Muslim Arabs to carry war-horses on raids overseas. It was larger and slower than a fighting galley but could carry less cargo than a merchant ship. Yet taridas were able to land men and horses, including fully armoured knights, right onto an enemy beach. They could also defend themselves if attacked at sea. Such galleys, taridas and merchant ships brought men, horses and food to the Crusaders in the Holy Land.

1 **Merchant ship or 'round ship'**
2 **Chain across harbour mouth**
3 **Winch to raise or lower chain**
4 **Tarida**
5 **Loading door, sealed with pitch during the voyage**
6 **Horses in canvas cradles to support them during the voyage**
7 **Oarsmen (all free men, not slaves)**

NAVAL BATTLES

Naval fights usually started with bows and crossbows being shot from a distance, trying to wound the enemy crew. A captain would try to get his ship alongside the enemy ship, so that the knights and sergeants who formed his fighting marines could rush across and try to capture the enemy vessel and its cargo intact.

A merchant ship is attacked by two sleek galleys on this 13th-century painted panel from Catalonia. All the ships are crowded with armoured knights.

URBAN KNIGHTS

After the Crusader states in the Middle East lost most of their territory to the Muslims, they were left only with the seaports and a narrow strip of land on the coast. Most knights now lived in these coastal cities and so they had to rely on money fiefs. These included sugar cane factories (below) that were often worked by Muslim slaves whose only chance of escape was to convert to Christianity.

Some knights had always lived in towns, particularly in southern Europe. In Italy these urban knights were a major political as well as military force. Knights commanded most city militias, but they also dominated many town councils – at least until the merchant class grew rich enough to challenge the knights' power. Other knightly families went into war as a business; they hired themselves and their followers out as ready-made armies to whoever paid the most.

MONEY FIEFS

Many kings and barons did not have enough land to give all their knights fiefs or estates, so those who were rich enough offered 'money fiefs' instead. Basically these were just a way in which a knight could raise the cash he needed to live and to pay for his expensive arms, armour, war-horse and servants. Money fiefs could be taxes on a weekly market, tolls for the use of a bridge or ferry, or money made from a factory or other business. Knights who lived in towns or cities were, of course, more likely to have money fiefs than knights who lived in the countryside.

MERCHANT KNIGHTS

Experience of naval warfare and military service overseas could also be useful for a knight thinking of earning extra money as a part-time merchant. Some even worked in the slave trade (see quotation above right) that flourished in parts of Europe.

At the same time, many rich merchant families bought themselves aristocratic status by lending money to a ruler who could make them into knights but who happened to be short of money. In Italy, these knights often lived in fortified houses in rich merchant cities rather than castles.

THE BUSINESS OF WAR

The most obvious business for any knight, whether he lived in a town or the countryside, was the mercenary business, fighting for whoever would pay him. By the 14th century many rich cities, particularly in Italy, were run by merchants who preferred to hire ready-made armies rather than rely on local militias or have to fight as soldiers themselves. Successful mercenary leaders employed their own knights, squires and infantrymen to make up a 'company'.

COMPANY WARFARE

When one war was over, a mercenary company would either split up or march off in search of another conflict and another employer.

For example, the Catalan Great Company consisted of experienced Spanish warriors who hired themselves out to the Byzantine emperor following the end of a war in southern Italy. Eventually they carved out their own small state around Athens in Greece – a state that survived to the end of the Middle Ages.

Knights fought at sea as well as on land. Spanish and Italian knights were particularly skilled in warfare at sea, manning fleets of war-galleys, serving as marines aboard rich trading ships and turning to piracy when all else failed.

THE WHITE COMPANY

The most famous company in 14th-century Italy was the White Company led by Sir John Hawkwood, an English knight who learned his business fighting the French during the Hundred Years War. In fact the later battles of the Hundred Years War were not between Englishmen and Frenchmen fighting for their countries, but tough professionals who were more interested in keeping a profitable war going than in winning a final victory!

The rich merchant cities of Italy had their own urban knights, who lived in fortified houses rather than castles. Some owned tall torre (towers) inside the city walls. There were so many of these torre that some Italian cities, such as the little town of San Gimignano (above), were compared to forests.

The knights kept law-and-order within the city. However knights with different loyalties sometimes ended up fighting each other (below).

DECLINE OF THE KNIGHT

FULL-TIME SOLDIERS

By the 15th century, kings still needed soldiers who were full-time professionals. In nearly all countries the law still said that rulers could demand military service from their knights. But now most knights were country gentlemen, courtiers or government officials.

So what was the point of demanding military service when most knights were neither trained as soldiers nor very keen on fighting? From a king's point of view it made much more sense to hire professional mercenaries who would fight at any time of the year.

Most of the earliest illustrations of firearms do not look at all realistic. But the little cannon shown in the left-hand corner of this one was clearly based on reality. The barrel is held in a large block of wood that could be raised or lowered with pegs.

There were many reasons why knighthood declined towards the end of the Middle Ages. New weapons like steel-armed crossbows, gunpowder, cannons and eventually handguns were only a part of the story. In fact the technology of armour kept pace with the technology of weapons well into the 15th century.

The main cause of the knights' decline was the fact that western European civilization was changing and the feudal knight was now out of date.

In the 15th century, Swiss infantry defeated heavily armoured cavalry knights so regularly that they helped undermine the whole prestige of the knightly elite. Even the best-equipped Austrian and Burgundian knights seemed unable to deal with Swiss mountaineers armed with crossbows, handguns and heavy-bladed halberds (a combined spear and axe).

THE PEACEFUL KNIGHT

The change from fighting knight to peaceful village landlord and local keeper of the peace happened first in England. There were civil wars and rebellions, but during the 14th and early 15th centuries English armies did most of their fighting in other countries, particularly in France and the Netherlands.

Even in England a knight's younger sons often became soldiers, or mercenaries, or priests, since it was the eldest brother who inherited the family estate. As a result most of the leading soldiers were still knights, even if most knights were not soldiers. Knights were still the commanders of most armies.

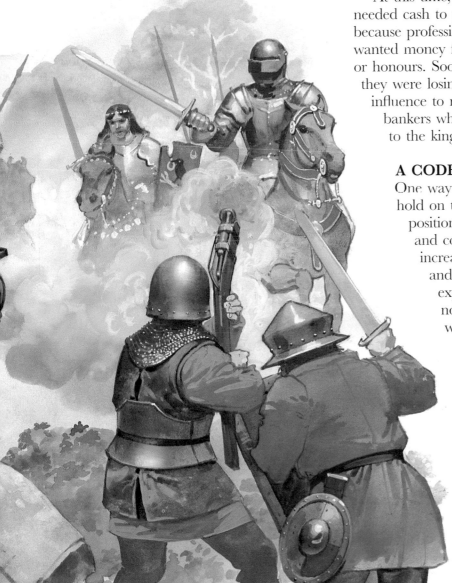

KNIGHTS UNDER THREAT

Even after the knights' military position had been undermined by full-time professional soldiers, the knights tried to stay part of the ruling class. However, in the 14th and 15th centuries, merchants and bankers, and even farmers, were getting richer than the knights.

At this time, kings and emperors needed cash to pay mercenary armies, because professional soldiers usually wanted money for their services, not fiefs or honours. Soon the knights found that they were losing their power and influence to rich merchants and bankers who were loaning money to the kings and emperors.

A CODE OF CHIVALRY

One way in which knights tried to hold on to their superior social position was to live extravagant and colourful lives. They wore increasingly elaborate clothes and jousted in hugely expensive tournaments where non-knightly 'commoners' were not allowed to take part, however rich they might be. In fact the traditional code of Courtly Love and chivalry, in which a knight put 'honour' above all things, had turned into a sort of dream world. It was like an expensive game that ruined many knightly families who felt they had to take part just to prove they were still the best.

Some huge cannons were made for siege warfare in the 15th century. One of the biggest was called 'Mons Meg', which is now kept in Edinburgh Castle in Scotland. Such giant guns were not, of course, used in open battle, where lighter forms of artillery were already threatening the future of the heavily armoured knight.

The threat from crossbows and hand-held guns forced the craftsmen of 15th-century western Europe to make this full plate armour (below). Lighter than the mixed mail and plate protection of the 14th century, a fit man could run, jump and even do somersaults in it!

The Middle Ages were a time of great turmoil in Europe. The armies of Popes, emperors, kings and barons fought each other for control of land and cities, and there were also wars between Christian knights and their pagan enemies.

800 Charlemagne, king of the Franks, crowned as Western Emperor. His miles become the first knights.
911 A band of Vikings are given the Duchy of Normandy to rule and settle (from then on called Normans).
955 Knights of Otto I of Germany defeat invading Magyars (Hungarians) at Battle of Lechfeld.
1066 Normans conquer England.
1071 Battle of Manzikert, Byzantines defeated by Turks.
1073 Start of major political conflicts between Popes and Western Emperors.
1096–1100 First Crusade conquers Jerusalem (1099), creation of Crusader States in the Middle East (Holy Land).
1147–1148 Second Crusade.
1173 New German expansion eastwards.
1187 Saracen ruler Saladin defeats the Crusader States and retakes Jerusalem.

1189–1192 Third Crusade.
1204 Fourth Crusade captures Byzantine capital of Constantinople.
1215 Magna Carta: King John makes political concessions to English barons.
1240 Mongol armies conquer Russia.
1241 Mongols invade eastern and central Europe. Teutonic, German and Polish knights defeated at Battle of Liegnitz. Hungarian army defeated.
1242 Teutonic Knights defeated at Battle of Lake Peipus.
1250 Collapse of Western Emperor's power in Germany and Italy.
1300 Mercenary armies becoming more common, especially in Italy.
1326 Drawing of early cannon appears in European manuscript.
1337 Start of Hundred Years War between England and France.
1348 Black Death (plague) ravages Europe.
1380 Lithuania finally accepts Christianity.
1415 England renews war with France, Battle of Agincourt.
1453 English expelled from France (except Calais), end of Hundred Years War.
1492 Spaniards conquer Muslim Granada, end of the Reconquista.
1798 Knights Hospitallers surrender Malta to Napoleon Bonaparte.

By the end of the Middle Ages jousting tournaments took place in some odd places and for some strange reasons. There were even jousts on Old London Bridge, though what the busy merchants of the City thought about this remains unknown! Sometimes whole teams would dress up as Turks, Saracens, Moors, pagan Greek gods or even monsters. It was all very different from the grim and dangerous military training of the 12th century.

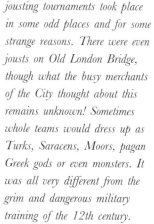

Glossary

allegiance: loyalty to a person or cause.
armourer: craftsman who makes armour.
Carolingian: ruling dynasty descended from Charlemagne.
chansons de geste: epic poems of heroic deeds.
coat-of-arms: heraldic pattern used by an individual or a family.
coif: head-covering, either of mail as a form of armour, or of cloth for civilian use.
conrois: close-packed unit of knights.
couched: held tightly under the armpit.
Courtly Love: ideal of love between a knight and his lady, expressed in terms of brave actions, music and poetry.
destrier: specially bred war-horse.
Feudal System: theoretic system whereby the military elite protected the peasants in return for food and taxes.
fief: piece of land or estate, given by a lord in return for military service.
fleurs-de-lys: heraldic flower, badge of the French royal family.
hauberk: mail coat, early form of armour.
heraldry: recognized system of colours and patterns used in coats-of-arms.
illuminated: decorated with pictures.
mail: form of armour consisting of many iron rings linked together.
mangonel: stone-throwing siege engine.
melée: 'free-for-all' combat between two groups, units or teams of cavalry.
mercenary: soldier hired for money.
miles: Latin word for knight.
Military Orders: religious order recruited from trained knights, similar to monks, but serving as elite troops.
militia: part-time soldiers, usually raised from the citizens of a town or city.
minstrel: singer, poet and song-writer.
money fief: source of income given by a ruler to a knight instead of a land fief.
Peace of God: one of several movements started by the Church in the 11th century to bring law and order back to chaotic parts of western Europe.
penance: penalty or form of sacrifice imposed by the Church on a sinner.
plate armour: armour made from relatively large, rigid pieces of metal.
pommel: the knob at the end of a sword hilt or handle, or raised front of a saddle.
Saracen: medieval name for an Arab rather than a Turkish Muslim.
squire: lowest rank of noble society, often a young man who has not been knighted.
stirrups: metal loops into which a horseman puts his feet.

Quotations

Most of the quotations are taken from medieval histories called chronicles, or from poems. The challenge to single combat on page 23 was made during the Hundred Years War between England and France. The oath on page 36 was made by a new recruit to the Order of Teutonic Knights. The quotation on the slave trade on page 43 is from the records of Genoa's legal advisor in the Black Sea port of Kaffa.

INDEX

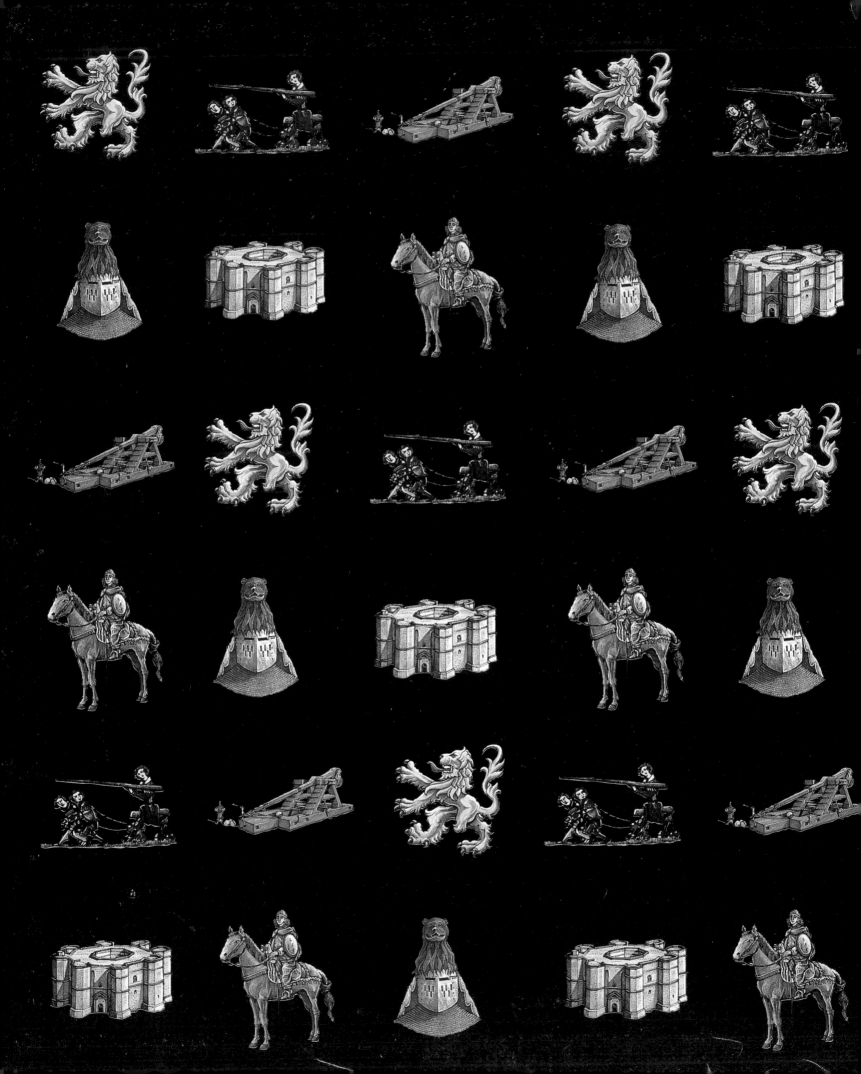